A catalogue record for this book is available from the National Library of Australia

Copyright © 2019 Hildegard Grivell

All rights reserved worldwide.

No part of the book may be copied or changed in any format, sold, or used in a way other than what is outlined in this book, under any circumstances, without the prior written permission of the publisher.

Publisher:
ASPG (Australian Self Publishing Group)
P.O. Box 159, Calwell, ACT Australia 2905
Email: publishaspg@gmail.com
http://www.inspiringpublishers.com

National Library of Australia Cataloguing-in-Publication entry

Author: *Grivell, Hildegard*

Title: **An Anthology of the Soul**/*Hildegard Grivell.*

Designed by Surendra Gupta

ISBN: 978-1-925908-33-6 (pbk)
        978-1-925908-34-3 (eBook)

Introduction

In our time, the word soul is referred to frequently and diversely. Soul experience, soul travel, soul food, soul journey, soul music are some of the terms we encounter, to name a few. In essence what is known about the human soul, her origin, her nature, her individuality, her destiny? Dictionairies define the soul as 'the principle of life, feeling, thought and action in humans, regarded as a distinct entity separate from the body ... the spiritual part of humans'. Is our soul the mirror of God? Is the soul the rejected feminine we seek to feel whole?

Philosophers from antiquity, mystics of the world's religions, theologians, psychologists and modern scientists have written about the soul and acknowledged her existence. The soul is also referred to by the Greek term psyche, and the Latin, anima. Like Spirit, the soul is an essential part of ourselves, the feminine polarity, of Spirit the masculine counterpart. During her sojourn on earth the soul seeks the bonding with Spirit, the fulfillment of her divine plan, the fulfillment of the law of love. The soul evolves through our free will decisions in our experiences of life.

Some modern psychologists and writers in spirituality have dubbed the soul our 'inner child' or referred to the soul as 'the forcefield of our being'. Our soul needs to be recognised, nurtured, loved and seen for who she is, essentially creative, spontaneous, joyful, resourceful, imaginative. Despite of these qualities, she may be burdened by traumas and sufferings experienced more recently or in the distant past. Our soul may need healing before she can attain the mystical union of soul with Spirit, freedom, peace, and enlightenment.

The soul enters into peace;
the Lord gives it peace
through his presence,
as He did to the just man, Simeon.
All the faculties are stilled;
the soul realises that it is now
very close to God,
without use of the outward senses.
If it were a little closer,
it would become one within in union.
Theresa of Avila

Let the soul blossom freely! Let the soul fear not to unfold her pedals! Let the soul fear not to enter God! Let the soul fear not the entering of God unto herself. Let the soul fear not the divine lover, to be wooed and to be loved, to be assimilated, to be reborn again.

Lady Master Nada

Hildagard

We have not turned our attention to the needs of the soul. We have not considered what is required by the soul in order to be healthy. We have not studied the soul, or sought to help it attain what is necessary to its evolution and its health. Because we have been five-sensory, we have focused upon the body and the personality. We have developed an extensive knowledge of the physical apparatus that the soul assumes when it incarnates.

Garry Zukav

Hildagard

Every soul is a celestial Venus to every other soul.

Ralph Waldo Emerson

Oh soul at rest, return unto your Lord, well satisfied, accepted.

R. Otto

My soul doth magnify the Lord, and my spirit hath rejoiced in God my Saviour.

St. Luke. 1:46-47

The soul that is full of wisdom is saturated with the spray of a bubbling fountain – God himself.

Hildegard of Bingen

Truly my soul waiteth upon God : from him cometh my salvation.

Psalm 62:1

At death, we will put off the body, as we put off our clothes when we lie down. The soul is the man; the body is only the clothes.

Matthew Henry

Do not despair, my soul, for hope has manifested itself; the hope of every soul has arrived from the unseen.

Rumi

Ingratitude is an enemy of the soul.

St. Bernard

Thou canst not discover the bounds of the soul, albeit thou pacest its every road, so deep is its foundation.
Heracleitus

The soul dwells within us, a flame the size of a thumb. When it is known as the Lord of the past and the future, then ceases all fear. This in truth is That.
Katha Upanishad

For more than ever I understand how close I must be to God if I wish to bring souls to Him.
Mother Theresa

In silence and in stillness a devout soul profiteth, and learned the hidden things of the Scriptures.
Thomas a' Kempis

Just as in this body the embodied soul must pass through childhood, youth and age, so too (at death) will he take another body up. In this a thoughtful man is not perplexed.
Bhagavad-Gita

But the love of the soul is love supreme.
It is love in our spiritual essence and of our eternal belonging.
Daphne Rose Kingma

Hildagard

An Anthology of the Soul

It is to this divine goodness that the soul most dutyfully and confidently commits itself for help and success in the difficult task of self – purification. When this has been accomplished, that is, when the soul will be free of all corruption and purified of all its stains, then at last it possesses in utter joy and has no fear whatever for itself nor any anxiety for any reason. This, then, is the fifth level. For it is one thing to achieve purity, another to be in posession of it, and the activity by which the soul restores the sullied state to purity and that by which it does not suffer itself to be defiled again are two entirely different things. On this level it conceives in every way how great it is in every respect; and when it has understood that, then with unbounded and wonderous confidence it advances toward God, that is, to the immediate contemplation of truth; and it attains that supreme and transcendent reward for which it has worked so hard.

St. Augustine

Fundamentally, the office of parenthood is to be the privileged means (and, indeed, it should be considered as divinely privileged) of enabling a soul to contact this world for the sake of evolution. If properly understood, there is probably no greater opportunity offered to mankind than this, to be the agent of the physical birth of a soul and to have the care of the young personality during the first few years of its existence on earth.

Eduard Bach

Sunset, Goals of the Soul

So it came about that I was able to see with absolute certainty that it was easier for us get to know God than to know our own soul. For our soul is so deeply set in God, and so greatly valued, that we cannot come to know it until we first know God, its Creator, to whom it is joined. Julian of Norwich The soul is not physical, yet it is the forcefield of our being.
Gary Zukav and Linda Francis

The soul knows that there is an inner Master.

Mark Prophet

No one soul is led in exactly the same way.

Jennifer Moorcroft
in Teresa of Avila

How close is your soul to my soul ! For what thing you are thinking, I know.

Rumi

The soul is Brahman, the Eternal. It is made of consciousness and mind: it is made of life and vision. It is made of the earth and the waters: it is made of air and space. It is made of light and darkness: It is made of desire and peace. It is made of virtue and vice. It is made of all that is near: it is made of all that is afar. It is made of all.

The Supreme
Teaching Upanishads

Let the soul in all courage be willing now to place that substance into the flame, to become a spherical reality of Being, a white sphere of light that is a golden sun held in the hands of Maitreya.

Lord Maitreya

In our soul we are conscious of the transcendental truth in us, the Universal, the Supreme Man; and this soul, the spiritual self, has its enjoyment in the renunciation of the individual self for the sake of the supreme soul.

Rabindranath Tagore

The real peace of the Soul and mind is with us when we are making spiritual advance, and it cannot be obtained by the accummulation of wealth alone, no matter how great.
Edward Bach

After all, the soul is something out of the common. While everything else that exists takes up a certain amount of room, the soul cannot be located in space.
C.G.Jung

The soul, then, remains a fallen potential that must be imbued with the reality of Spirit, purified through prayer and supplication and returned to the glory from which it descended and to the unity of the Whole.
El Morya

He who does good to his own soul also does good to the souls of his friends.
Brother Giles

But the soul he has made not merely like the image of Himself, or like anything proceeding from Himself that is predicated of Him, but He has made her like Himself, in fact like everything that He is – like His nature, His essence and His emanating – immanent activity, and like the ground wherein He subsides in Himself, where he ever bears His only – begotten Son and where the Holy Ghost blossoms forth: it is like this outflowing, indwelling work that God has formed the soul.
Meister Eckhart

Hildagard

Hildagard

As the soul rises to the level of her Holy Christ Self and then to the level of her I Am Presence, she becomes a luminary, lighting the way that others might follow the star of Christ's appearing within themselves. She opens their eyes that they may see his star, be his star, ingest his light, be possessed by his light, become his light, exult Christ and be exulted in him. In order for the ascending soul to be such a facilitator, she must be possessed of her God-control which mobilises the good in all life and leads her companions on the straight and narrow way of self-mastery.

Kuthumi

Impression is as an imprint in the soul. For the soul, like a ring or seal, received the appropriate imprint of those things that each of the senses introduces. The mind like wax receives the imprint and preserves it in sharp clarity, until forgetfulness, memory's antagonist, smooths away the imprint and renders it faint or completely obliterates it. But the object that had appeared, and made the impression at times renders the soul well disposed at other times the revers. This affection of the soul is called impulse, which has been defined as the initial movement of the soul.

Philo of Alexandria

The entire effort of our Soul is to become God. This effort is as natural to man as that of flying is to the birds.

Marsilio Ficino

Don't let temptations frighten you. They are the trials of those souls whom God wants to put to the test when He sees them strong enough to sustain the battle, weaving with their own hands, the crown of glory.

Padre Pio

The soul, then, is a being of light, a sphere of white fire, with the colourations, auric colourations, that mark the choices of free will.

Lanello

I am the lover of thy soul.

Lord Maitreya

I believe that the soul's proper abode, to put it that way, and its homeland, is God Himself by whom it has been created.

St. Augustine

Our soul reposes in God its true rest, and stands in God, its true strength, and is fundamentally rooted in God, its eternal love. So if we want to come to know our soul, and enjoy its fellowship as it were, it is necessary to seek it in our Lord in whom it is enclosed.

Julian of Norwich

Thou shalt love the Lord thy God with all thy heart, and with all thy soul, and with all thy mind.

Matthew 23:37

The souls of man see their images as if in the mirror of Dionysus, and come down to that level with a leap from above: but they are not cut off from their principle and their Nous: They have gone on ahead of it down to earth, but their tops are firmely set above in heaven.

Plotinus

I can find nothing with which to compare the great beauty of a soul and its great capacity.

Teresa of Avila

Through the path of initiation, the soul can indeed attain that soul liberation that is desired as the deep desiring of God within to be God.

Kwan Yin

The intellect cannot take the place of our soul. That is why the education of the heart and soul is just as important as the education of the mind. To create a safe harbor for the soul, we sometimes have to turn off the intellect and consciously enter into the heart and soul to get in touch with our inner creative self.

Elisabeth Clare Prophet

As an individual soul, you remain an individual soul. You are both individual and one with all that is.

Garry Zukav

Description of the Soul

Thus the soul when it shall have driven away from itself all that is contrary to the Divine Will, becomes transformed in God in love ... the soul then becomes immediately enlightened by and transformed in God because He communicates his own supernatural being in such a way that the soul seems to be God Himself and to possess the things of God ... the soul seems to be God rather than itself and indeed is God rather than itself and indeed is God by participation.

St. John of the Cross

The beautiful souls are they that are universal, open and ready for all things. Montaigne *For what is a man profited, if he shall gain the whole world, and lose his own soul.*

Matthew 16:26

An Anthology of the Soul

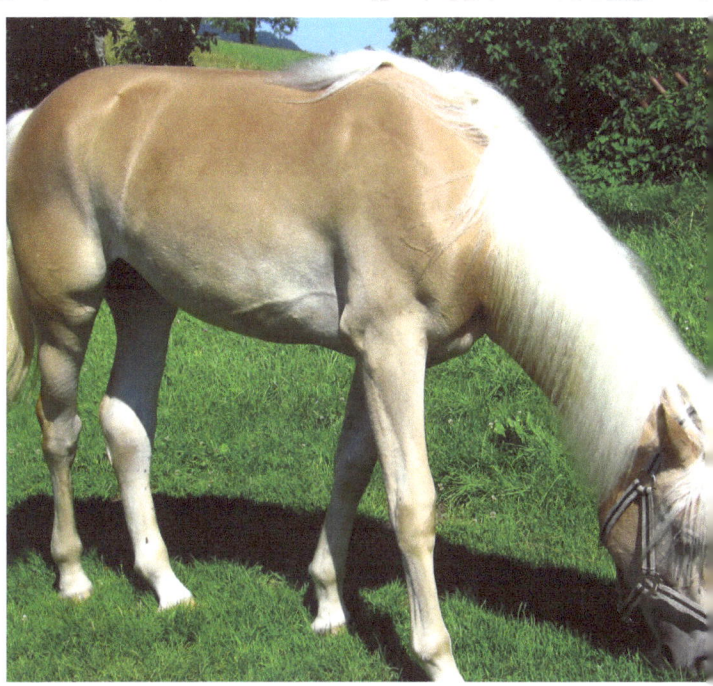

Hildagard

Had there been a new soul created for each of the countless milliards of human beings that have passed away, and had there been no reincarnation – it would become difficult indeed to provide room for the disembodied 'spirits'.

H.P. Blavatsky

It is this God alone, then, who is to be adored by the soul, without reservation and without confusion. Clearly, whatever the soul adores as God, it necessarily considers more excellent than itself; and neither the earth, nor the seas, nor the stars, nor the moon, nor the sun, nor anything at all that can be touched or seen with our eyes, nor even heaven itself, invisible to us, are to be considered superior to the nature of the soul. In fact, reason proves conclusively that all these are far inferior to a single soul, if lovers of the truth will but muster the courage to follow its leadership with the great constancy and devotion over paths that prove rugged for being little traveled.

St. Augustine

The conscious path to authentic power requires recognition of the nonphysical dimensions of the human being, of the soul, and a growing knowledge of what the soul is and what it wants.

Gary Zukav

God cannot understand Himself without the soul nor the soul without God – so completely are they one.

Meister Eckhart

Ultimately all the souls have to develop all their powers, but the order in which these powers are developed depends on the circumstances amid which the soul is placed. Climate, the fertility or sterility of Nature, the life of the mountain or of the plain, of the inland forest or the ocean shore – these things and countless others will call into activity one set or another of the awakening mental energies. A life of extreme hardship, of ceaseless struggles with Nature, will develop very different powers from those evolved amid the luxuriant plenty of a tropical island; both sets of powers are needed, for the soul is to conquer every region of Nature, but striking differences may thus be evolved even in souls of the same age, and one may appear to be more advanced than the other, according as the observer estimates most highly, the more practical or the more 'contemplative' powers of the soul, the active outward-going energies, or the quiet inward-turned musing faculties. The perfected soul possesses all, but the soul in the making must develop them successively, and thus arises, another cause of the immense variety found among human beings.

Annie Besant

Let every soul be subject unto the higher powers.
For there is no power but of God.

Romans 13:1

A soul cannot see the light so long as she fixes her gaze upon the darkness.

St.Bernard

The soul's journey isn't a game, a chase, or a gamble. It follows a predetermined course toward the moment of waking up.

Deepak Chopra

As in this world of art, so in the spiritual world, our soul waits for its freedom from the ego to reach that disinterested joy which is the source and goal of creation.

Rabindranath Tagore

The soul is only as strong as its works.

Hildegard of Bingen

Thou hast in love of my soul delivered it from the pit of corruption: for thou hast cast all my sins behind thy back.

Isaiah 38:17

When the soul talks, you can't help but listen, and the words it speaks arise spontaneously from no location and from no earlier time.

Fred Alan Wolf

An Anthology of the Soul

Why art thou cast down, O my soul? and why art thou disquieted within me? Hope thou in God: for I shall yet praise him, who is the health of my countenance, and my God.
Psalm 42:11

Hildagard

The first way in which God speaks to us is in the essence of the soul, which no creature can penetrate nor in which any creature can speak, for God alone dwells there, and he alone can speak there, the soul takes leave of all things, all of its faculties fall silent and it glimpses the ground of its bare essence. And in this bareness and silence God speaks his word and the soul hears it. And this voice of God is nothing other than an inward sense of God within us, which springs forth from God into the essence of our soul and overflows all its faculties, causing such joy that we would gladly be free of all our own activity and allow God alone to work in the essence of our soul.

Meister Eckhart

The soul, in which the power will become stronger than the counterfeit spirit, is strong and it flees from evil and through the intervention of the incorruptible one, it is saved and it is taken up to the rest of the aeons.

The Apocryphon of John
Nag Hammadi Library

Hildagard

The individual unit of evolution is the soul. This perception is new to us because, as a species, we have not before been aware of the existence of the soul. In our religious thoughts we acknowledge what we call the soul, but we have not until now, taken it seriously enough to consider what the existence of the soul means in terms of everyday experience, in terms of the joys and pains and sorrows and fulfillments that make a human life.

Gary Zukav

The cleansing of the soul is to regain the newness of her former nature and to turn herself back again.

The Exegesis on the Soul
Nag Hammadi Library

Each soul is the hostage of its own deeds.

The Koran

Life is God living and working in the soul; death is the soul living and working according to the sense and reason of bestial flesh and blood.

William Law

The soul is sensitive and impressionable, and although we dont consciously remember all the experiences we've had in all of our embodiments, our soul does. This includes unpleasant experiences where our soul was wounded. When we go through physical or emotional trauma, we dont just feel it in our body or in our emotions, we feel it in our soul as well.

Elisabeth Clare Prophet

An Anthology of the Soul

For the soul that comes to heaven is precious to God, and the place is so holy that the goodness of God will never allow the soul who gets there to have sinned without that sin being compensated. Ever known it is blessedly made good by God's surpassing worth.

Julian of Norwich

In every exposition of the Perennial Philosophy the human soul is regarded as feminine in relation to the Godhead.

Aldous Huxley

The universe lies in soul which bears it up, and nothing is without a share of soul.

Plotinus

The soul that is attached to anything, however much good there may be in it, will not arrive at the liberty of the divine union. For whether it be a strong wire rope or a slender and delicate thread that holds the bird, it matters not, if it really holds it fast; for until the cord be broken, the bird cannot fly. So the soul, held by the bounds of human affections, however slight they may be, cannot, while they last, make its way to God.

St. John of the Cross

The earth is to the sun, as the soul is to God.

Hildegard of Bingen

Your soul evolves in eternity.

Gary Zukav

An Anthology of the Soul

The reason for the descent of the soul to earthly existence is to experience the trials of life. The soul of man has to be strengthened by test, ordeal and confrontation with physical reality .... It is very difficult if not impossible, to make progress any other way. The very essence of trial is a process of releasing the holy spark in harsh reality.

Adin Steinsaltz

The souls are suffering the pangs of hunger, yet the fruit of knowledge is more plentiful than the stones of the valleys.

Kahlil Gibran

Renunciation, temptations, struggles, persecutions, and all kinds of sacrifices are what surround the soul that has opted for holiness.

Mother Teresa

The soul is tripartite, one part reasoning, a second spirited, a third desiderative.

Philo of Alexandria

Man must find his own Soul. He who has found and knows his Soul has found all the worlds, has achieved all his desires.

Chandogya Upanishad

Let souls be drawn together, then, according to their highest calling in God. Let magnanimous hearts unite in service. For their delight in the law of God can overcome the karmic conditions that would otherwise pit them against one another.

Kuthumi

Thus the soul worketh all its works in God: nay, thus doth God work His own work in it, so that it is not so much the soul who worketh, as that the soul itself is the work of God.

Gerlac Petersen

Transformation and Transcendence of the soul

An Anthology of the Soul

Your soul is sensitive, intuitive, fragile.
Your soul is your inner child.

Elisabeth Clare Prophet

The soul that loves God lives more in the next life than in this, because it lives rather where it loves than where it dwells.

St. John of the Cross

In that direction whither every night the soul departs, then in the time of the dawn He brings back the soul.

Rumi

Until you have found God in your own soul, the whole world will seem meaningless to you.

Kabir

That soul must be very special and very important to God – in fact, of ultimate importance. For why should the God of very god's sponser a soul if that soul has no chance, no something within that can spring forth as a flower, even as a shoot pushes up through the crusty earth?

Rathnasambhava

The soul cannot tolerate brutality. It cannot tolerate abundancies of pain and irrationality. It cannot tolerate being lied to. ... It cannot tolerate non-forgiveness. It cannot tolerate jealousies and hatreds. These are contaminants, poisons, for it.

Gary Zukav

And in my solitude I thought of Him and followed these two streams in His heart. Upon the banks of the one I met my own soul; and sometimes my own soul was a begger and a wanderer, and sometimes it was a princess in her garden.

Kahlil Gibran

The desire of our soul is to thy name, and to the rememberence of thee. With my soul have I desired thee.

Isaiah 26. 8:9

God teaches by pouring light into the soul of the learner and illuminating the mind with the true light, his own Word. And even though we are taught by just men who have received the grace of teaching, it is still the Lord who teaches us through them.

Origin of Alexandria

Thus the soul, since it is immortal and has been born many times, and has seen all things both here and in the other world, has learned everything that is.

Plato

For a moment now, imagine yourself as an egoless being. Imagine yourself not being concerned about what others think of you, having no thoughts or opinions of others but only the freedom to acknowledge the Light, to bow to the Atman within and to treasure a soul to whom God has given the vessel of body and mind.

Rathnasambhava

Hildagard

Hildagard

Hildagard

But if a man has preserved his innocence and joins to it humility, does he not seem to you to possess a twofold beauty of soul?

St. Bernard

My soul is exeeding sorrowful unto death.

Mark 14 : 34

The eyes of the body are but the smallest part of the soul.

Philo of Alexandria

All the powers of the soul belong to the soul alone as their principle. But some powers belong to the soul alone as their subject: such are intellect and will. These powers must remain in the soul after the destruction of the body.

St. Thomas Aquinas

'Soul' in itself implies self conscious life. It is the seat of his emotions, desires, affections.

Footnote in Genesis

Soul, saith Christ, thou shalt be mine whilst I am in heaven; and Lord, saith the soul, I will be thine whilst I am on earth. I will never leave thee nor forsake thee, saith Christ: O my Lord, saith the soul, hold me fast in thy hand, that I may never leave nor forsake thee; ... The espousals betwixt Christ and the soul are for ever.

John Flavel

Do not abandon your soul to temptation, says the Holy Spirit, because the joy of the heart is the life of the soul, it is an inexhaustible treasure of sanctity; while sadness is the slow death of the soul it is of no use to anyone.

Padre Pio

Softly and quietly I come into the soul. As the breath of live is received by a new born child, so the soul receives the infusion, the grace of the Holy Spirit. For I represent the influx of Father – Mother God, twin flames of Alpha and Omega, as the cloven tongues of Paraclete descend to quicken your souls, to quicken your consciousness, to quicken the light manifestation.

Maha Chohan

All things of which this world is composed, as the soul and the body, will return to the principle and to the root from which they sprang. For God is the beginning and He is the end of all the degrees of creation. And all the degrees are bound with His seal. He is the unique Being, in spite of the innumerable forms in which He is clothed.

Rabbi Simeon bar Yohai

And when you allow your soul to merge with that Christ Self, you become the bride of Christ who is worthy to enter the wedding feast and remain with the bridegroom for ever.

Kim Michaels

Hildagard

Hildagard

O soul how long wilt thou sleep and how often wilt thou wake?

Ràbi a of Basra

There is no salvation of the soul, or hope of everlasting life, but in the cross. Take up therefore your cross and follow Jesus, (Luke 14:27), and you shall go into life everlasting.

Thomas a'Kempis

O soul, before the world was I longed for thee: and I still long for thee and thou for me. Therefore, when the two desires unite, Love shall be fulfilled.

Mechthild of Magdeburg

Wisdom is sweet for your soul; if you find it there is a future hope for you, and your hope will not be cut off.

Proverbs 24:14

How shall you then understand Jesus of Nazareth, a man simple and alone, who came without armies or ships, to establish a kingdom in the heart and an empire in the free spaces of the soul?

Kahlil Gibran

In nurishing the soul and embracing the One can you do it without letting them leave?

Lao - Tzu

Humanity is small in stature, but powerful in strength of soul.

Hildegard of Bingen

The soul is not made one with the Word of God and joined with Him until such a time as all the winter of her personal disorders and the storm of her vices has passed so that she no longer vacillates and is carried about with every kind of doctrine. When, therefore, all these things have gone out of the soul, and the tempest of desires has fled from her, then the flowers of the virtues can begin to burgeon in her ... Then also will she hear the voice of 'the turtle-dove', which surely denotes that wisdom which the steward of the Word speakes among the perfect, the deep wisdom of God which is hidden in mystery.

Origin of Alexandria

The beloved of my heart is the guest of my soul.

Al-Ghazáli in Ihyá

The road to your soul is through your heart.

Gary Zukav

Those who leave this world and have not found their soul, and that love which is Truth, find not their freedom in other worlds. But those who leave this world and have found their soul and that love which is Truth, for them there is the liberty of the Spirit, in this world and in the world to come.

Chandogya Upanishad

I've still to meet a teacher who hasn't lived through many, many dark nights of the soul.

Louise Hay

The soul has its seasons just the same as the year. It too must pass through life's autumn of dying, a desolate period of heart-hurt and crying, followed by winter in whose frostbitten hand my heart is as frozen as the snow-covered land yes, man too must pass through the seasons God sends, content in the knowledge that everything ends, and oh what a blessing to know there are reasons and to find that our soul must, too, have its seasons.

Helen Steiner Rice

Hildagard